Bitcoin:
Your Escape

Bitcoin: Your Escape
by Matt Haslem

First edition

Paperback: ISBN 978-0-6486457-6-4

Visit BitcoinYourEscape.com for copies.

Table of Contents

Your Escape Starts Here

You're trapped—every paycheck buys you less; every dollar siphoned from your account quicker. You shrug it off—heck, it's just how life works.

But deeper down, you know something's broken: your money is dying. Your dreams of a home, an early retirement, or a better life for your kids slip further with each crumbling dollar.

Year after year, you're chained to a system that only tightens its grip. Press on, and the bars close tighter—you sink deeper. Bitcoin is your escape.

This book isn't about what Bitcoin "is"—it's about scaling the mountain of obstacles that stand between you and a freer life. No jargon. No dry writing—just a battle-tested narrative that turns Bitcoin adoption into an epic, achievable climb instead of a technical slog. I'm here to show you the path up that mountain—the one I bloodied myself climbing so you don't have to.

I watched governments and central banks print 40% of all dollars in existence in just two years. Watched them water down every dollar I'd saved, making my hard work seemingly worthless.

But this went far beyond a loss of purchasing power—it stole the very notion of saving and building for the future. If our money loses its meaning, and saving feels pointless, it crushes our drive, our motivations, our dreams. Why bust ass, sacrificing, if the reward just evaporates?

Now I save in something no government can print, no bank can freeze, no politician can debase.

But the climb nearly killed me.

I got scammed. Panic sold the bottom. Bought shitcoins. Lost keys. Every possible fuck-up, I hit it face-first. Each scar taught me something, and I hammered those lessons into this book like iron rungs in sheer rock. This is your Via Ferrata—your somewhat protected climbing route through the chaos.

Fair warning: This climb will test you. Scammers lurk at every ledge. The media will scream you're insane. Your family will think you've joined a cult. Markets will tank 50% while you're still learning the ropes.

You'll want to quit. Everyone does. The system trained you to stay down, trust the experts, follow the herd. But you're reading this because some part of you knows that's bullshit. That same part will get you to the summit—if you're willing to climb.

Your escape starts now. Not tomorrow when conditions are perfect. Now—while your dollars still hold any value at all.

Clip in, drop the dead weight, and climb—the summit's waiting.

"Most people are slaves and don't even know it."

—Saifedean Ammous

Chapter 1: The Escape Begins

You felt it first at the grocery store—same paycheck, smaller cart. Then at the gas pump—sixty bucks used to fill the tank, now it barely gets you halfway. Your landlord's "minor" rent increase somehow swallowed your entire raise.

The trap revealed itself in small thefts. Death by a thousand cuts. Most people adjust. Shrug. Work more hours. You?

You stopped.

Just long enough to see through the bullshit. The promise you'd bought into—work hard, save money, retire secure—was breaking apart in your hands. Raw. Sharp. Undeniable.

That wasn't supposed to happen.

You were meant to keep your head down. Trust the system. Follow the plan. Do what you're told, and hope it all works out.

But the moment you recognize the chains—your escape has already begun.

In your gut, you already know the solution. That thing you've dismissed a million times. Massive and obvious, but you ignored it, wrote it off, rolled your eyes at it... until now. Now you need it. Bitcoin. The thing that doesn't give a shit about your government's money printer.

And there it is—the mountain. Rising between you and that escape. The brutal climb you've avoided. Treacherous, unforgiving, but the only path out of this trap. At the top, a flicker of orange burns through the mist. Distant. Elusive. Free.

It sparks something raw inside you. The truth hits: your retirement statement's a joke. That house? Never happening. Time with your kids? Stolen while you grind for devaluing paper. The system already spent your future. But that orange glow—that's real. That's the way out. Not just to wealth, but to time you control, choices you make, a life no one can devalue.

"Good!" You startle at my voice. Turn to find me standing there—rope slung over my shoulder, my jacket shredded and face bruised as if I'd freshly crawled from a car wreck just moments ago.

"I see you've broken from the pack—no time for introductions; just keep up."

I toss you the rope. 'You'll need this.'

You catch it hesitantly, your gaze flicking over my kit—harness, carabiners, boots still caked from yesterday's climb.

“Been watching you circle the base of this mountain for years. Now that you're finally looking up, you'll want to climb.”

"The path looks worn?" you stutter out.

My boot slides into one of the crushed footprints—"trampled by thousands over the years, all chasing that same dream.”

“But people do escape, right?”

“Some tried. A few clawed close, only to slip. The rest?” I point downward. “Look.”

You follow my gesture. Crushed stone, dust, bone—wallets drained by scams, seed phrases lost to forgetfulness, fortunes panic-sold at the first obstacles. Buying was never their problem; gripping through the blizzards was. They thought they’d break free. Instead, they became the very path you tread.

"You sure you want this?" I ask. "The mountain doesn't care. It'll bury you too if you freeze."

"I'm doing this for me," you mutter, voice low and edged. "I'm grinding harder than ever, pouring it all in, but I'm stuck—worse, slipping back. I'm done—I'm breaking out."

Your fists clench, nails biting skin. The mountain's orange gleam catches your eye—igniting something fierce and raw inside you.

"Good. Channel that," I say, watching your transformation. "But keep moving. First rule up here: stagnate, and you become part of the mountain. Another frozen warning."

You scan the path ahead. "This doesn't look so hard. Why do people fail?"

"That's what they all think," I reply. "Until they hear it."

"Hear what?"

I hold up a hand for silence. "Listen. Your first obstacle—it's already here."

You strain to hear. At first, nothing. Dead silence. Then something faint, like whispers carried on wind.

"I don't—" you start, then freeze. The voices hit you all at once, clear as if they're standing right behind you.

Your boss: “Don't throw away stability.”
Your mom: “Remember Uncle Jerry’s investments? This is exactly like his pet rocks.”
Your friends: “Crypto's a scam, bro.”

The voices drag at your boots like quicksand.

They mean well—that's what makes it worse. They're not evil, just infected with the same disease that's kept you from climbing all this time. Fear dressed up as wisdom. Caution marketed as love. They call it risky, because they’ve never been free. And they'll suffocate you with 'protection' because watching you climb reminds them they never tried. Their comfort zone is your coffin.

The voices pull harder the moment you take a step. That's their secret—they get loudest when you actually move.

"Push through," I say. "If you want the Bitcoin summit, you'll have to unlearn everything that held you down. It starts right here, right now."

I point down at the base. The world you knew chugs along below—everyone busy with their routines, not even noticing you've started climbing.

"The higher you go, the quieter those voices get," I warn. "But here's what they don't tell you—the silence up here is worse. Those obstacles ahead? They'll make you beg to hear even those negative voices again. At least they were familiar."

The path narrows ahead. The air thins. A few other climbers move past us, but they're strangers—focused on their own battle with the mountain.

"Last chance," I say, watching you stare at that orange glow above. "Down there, you're trapped but not alone. Up here, you're free but the loneliness cuts deep. Your choice."

You look at the narrowing trail, back at your old life below, then up at the beckoning summit. Escape isn't a place. It's a decision.

Most never escape fiat—not because the mountain's too high, but because they never start the climb.
You move.

Climber's Check List

In Chapter 1, you first question the system and realize you can't keep living under the old rules. This is where your climb begins.

1. **My "Why Escape"**
    - Write down the exact moment you saw Bitcoin as your way out – maybe it was a bill you couldn't pay or a paycheck that shrank before your eyes. That single sentence is the fuel for your ascent.
    - Keep it front and center—when the climb gets steep, this reminder will pull you back on course.

2. **Prepare Your Gear**
    - Download a beginner-friendly crypto wallet (Exodus—only from the official site).
    - Sign up with a reputable exchange (Coinbase, CoinSpot, Kraken, or your local favorite) so you can grab your first sats the moment you're ready.

"The root problem with conventional currency is all the trust that's required to make it work."

—Satoshi Nakamoto

Chapter 2: The Weight You Carry

The voices fade, swallowed by a rising wind. Now it's just you and the mountain.

Yet something heavier pulls at your shoulders. You might have thought that cutting through everyone's doubts—ignoring the "Stay put!" warnings—was all it took to be free. You were wrong. The real battle is inside: decades of money myths and risk-averse reflexes pressing down on you like lead.

Drop it, or it'll drag you off a cliff—literally and metaphorically.

The pack cuts into your shoulders—unquestioned baggage handed to you at birth (congrats, here's your lifetime subscription). And you kept stuffing it.

And for the most part, it worked. The illusion held.

When everyone around you carries the same pack, no one questions the weight.

But now, for the first time, you stop. Dump it off.

You weren't even planning to. But the wind is cutting through, and you need to start a fire. You kneel in the snow, unzip the pack, and see what you've been carrying all this time.

At first, it's small stuff—beliefs drilled deep: the job is security, debt is a tool, the bank is king. You dump them in the snow—parents' words, teachers' rules, system's lies. No one asked: What if it's bullshit? Not them, not you—until now.

Then, at the bottom: a crisp hundred-dollar bill.

Down there, it was everything—rent, food, power. Up here?

You turn it over, tracing its thin, fragile threads.
Does this even have value? What made it worth a damn?

Years traded—hours torched, freedom bled—for this?

A chill crawls up your spine. They swore it meant security. You never questioned it. Everyone nodded, too scared to peek behind the curtain.

But it's crumbling—year by year, it buys less, holds less. Printed on whims, propped by trust—blind trust.

As fire consumes the bill, your throat tightens like a fist. Each curl of smoke carries fragments of your life—countless hours grinding at a desk, dreams deferred, moments with loved ones sacrificed—all for this paper now turning to ash. Fragile. Hollow. Worthless. The truth burns brighter than the flame: you traded irreplaceable time for something designed to die. Gone.

A shiver crawls through you—not from mountain cold, but from clarity's brutal awakening. The true weight dragging you down was never your job or your debt—it was believing the lie that their money was real, that their system worked for you, that there was no alternative. The system blinded you with green—but now this orange flame engulfing it, seems to guide you forward. Warmth. Energy. Truth.

The flames settle to embers. The dollar is ash.

You shoulder your pack—essentials only, lighter now, free of what never served you. You're not just moving; you're ascending. Your steps find new certainty on the trail, each footfall more confident than the last. The lingering smoke of that burned bill trails behind you, not as a loss, but as liberation—a final reminder of everything you've chosen to leave behind in your climb toward something unconfiscatable, uncensorable, and truly yours.

At a rocky outcrop, you rest, catching your breath. A woman trudges up—Maria, single mom, pack light, resolve determined. "I'm climbing for my kids," she says, voice steady. You share water, a quiet moment, both eyeing the peak. She moves on; her words stick, fueling your own stakes.

As I watch you reorganize your pack, I dig into mine. Pull out a folded scrap—orange, worn.

“Take it,” I say, thrusting it at you.

You unfold it—a Bitcoin flag, bold against the orange. Your brow lifts.

“Been with me since the start,” I grunt. “Would look good at the top, if we ever make it.”

You hesitate, offering it back. I shake my head.

Keep it. Lightens the load.

You tuck it deep, hands lingering on the promise.

The summit pull takes on a different sense. The climb shifts—lighter, freer—where Bitcoin’s weightless promise starts to make sense against the crushing burden you've carried all your life.

Climber's Check List

In Chapter 2, you confront old beliefs about money—heavy baggage you've been dragging from the system. You realize some of these "truths" might be holding you down instead of helping you climb.

1. **Unload Old Beliefs**
    - List **three** money beliefs you've carried your whole life (e.g., "Debt is normal," "A stable job is the only security," "Investing is too risky").
    - Next to each, jot down **why** it might no longer serve you now that you're climbing toward financial freedom.
2. **Burn the Dead Weight**
    - Choose **one** of those beliefs to challenge directly this week. Maybe you watch a short documentary on alternative finance, or read an article on why inflation erodes fiat savings.
    - The goal: **prove** to yourself that the old belief is holding you back—and start letting go.

"Don't trust, verify"

Chapter 3:
The Fake Guide

I hang back a few paces, letting you take the lead. For the first time since you started climbing, you feel lighter. The weight is gone. The doubts are quiet. And for the first time, this feels possible.

Then, just ahead on the trail, you see him.

He's short but strong, his frame built for this terrain. A natural-born climber.

The way he moves — effortless. Like the mountain bends to him.

"I presume you're both new to this," he says with a nod. "You don't have to do this alone."

I stay quiet, letting you make the choice. Waiting to hear the words.

You don't hesitate—"Thanks! Of course we want help!" You've spent your whole damn life being told what to do next.

From the moment you started school, the pattern was

locked in. Bell rings, you sit. Another bell rings, you march. Every step paved, every mistake padded.

"Go to school," they said. "Do well."
"Get a job," they said. "Climb the ladder."
"Save for retirement," they said. "Don't question the system."

You never learned to trust yourself—just to wait for instructions.

So now, on the mountain, when someone shows up all confident, all smooth, acting like they've done this a hundred times?

You don't think. You follow.

Because the truth is—deep down—you still want someone to nod and say:

"You're doing this right."

You want a parent, a teacher, a fucking YouTuber to take the wheel and steer you out of the chaos.

That's not weakness. It's just... human.
I know I did. Over and over.

I'd join exclusive Telegram groups promising insider info on the next "hot" coin—mods playing god, silencing anyone who questioned them.

YouTubers with thumbnails screaming "Five coins to buy right now." I had their notifications on like gospel.

One guy claimed he'd cracked the code—automated trading bots for "24/7 gains while you sleep." I jumped in. Set it up. Woke up to a drained stack by the morning. No refund. No apology. Just silence.

It wiped out every satoshi I'd scraped together working freelance, grinding for weeks to accumulate. That loss burned in my chest—a knot of dread I couldn't shake. I was furious at the "expert," at those YouTubers, but mostly at myself. Embarrassed—every boast to my mates about my "trading skills" now a punchline. I hated that I'd trusted someone else's hype.

Fact was, I wasn't investing—I was outsourcing responsibility. Still following. Still hoping someone else would do the thinking, the bleeding, the deciding. I wasn't climbing. I was being pulled—blind, desperate, and pretending it was progress.

At first, whoever shows up on your journey seems perfect—exactly the savior you were hoping for. Someone who's been here before. Someone who knows the way up.

"You can keep struggling on your own," he says, "or I can show you a better way." A faster way. A safer way. The right way. And it sounds tempting. You're new to this. He's experienced. Why wouldn't you follow? So you do.

Starting on his path, things feel easier. The bastard moves like he owns the place. No stumbles, no second guesses. Makes you feel like the idiot just for hesitating. Relief floods you—finally, someone who actually knows the terrain.

But then, slowly, things start to change.

- The path gets steeper.
- The footing becomes unstable.
- It's barely a trail at all.

"Are you sure this is the right way?" you ask.

"Trust me," he says. And for a while, you do. Until suddenly—he's gone.

You stop. You look around. He's nowhere to be found. No explanation. No warning. No sign of him at all. And now, you're stranded.

You followed him into this. And now, you have no idea how to get out. The path you thought was safe? It's a dead end. The shortcut? It was a trap.

The system trained you to follow — break that, or you'll just follow someone else off a cliff.

You were never his student. You were his product. The Fake Guide's game is simple: promise certainty, prey on fear, sell a shortcut that doesn't exist.

Our guide was draped in climbing gear. Yours might wear an expensive suit. Maybe they hold a bachelor's degree in finance, speak in polished soundbites, and have an office lined with books they never actually read.

Or maybe they go all glitz—head to toe in Gucci, flexing watches, cars, and an Instagram lifestyle that screams success.

Different costumes, same game.

Whatever image they sell is designed to make you believe they've figured it out. You just have to follow. But once you've paid, once you're invested—he's gone.

You turn to me and meet my knowing nod: not cocky, not angry, just a lesson best experienced.

The wind howls. You steady yourself. You understand the mistake. There was never a shortcut. No one can climb for you.

You draw a deep breath, face the path ahead, and study the terrain. No more blind trust. No more waiting for someone else to lead the way. You find your own footing. You choose your own steps. And slowly, carefully—you climb out.

By the time we reach solid ground again, you're different. The climb feels different. You've stopped looking for someone to show you the way. Because for the first time, you trust yourself.

Climber's Check List

In Chapter 3, you see how tempting it is to follow a self-proclaimed "expert" promising an easy way out. You learn it's better to trust yourself than chase shortcuts.

1. **Spot the Trap**
   o Write down three promises you've heard from financial 'gurus' (online or off). Cross out any that sound too good to be true—like 'double your money overnight.' That's your first filter for bullshit.
2. **Find A Solid Voice**
   o Pick one Bitcoin educator who's been around since before the hype, like Andreas Antonopoulos. Watch one talk or read one article, and jot down what feels different from the noise. Trust your gut—this is your compass now."

"Bitcoin is not smooth jazz—Bitcoin is punk rock."

—Andreas M. Antonopoulos

Chapter 4: The Fractured Path

Adopting Bitcoin is anything but a neat, steady, A to B journey.

The path up—utter chaos.

Every setback and pitfall makes you question your next step.

You'll stumble, backtrack, hit dead ends. Most don't make it—not because they're not clever, but because they're not stubborn enough to keep moving when the mountain tries to shake them off. It's grit that gets you higher—not luck, not smarts, not a perfect plan.

And with that, the trail suddenly forks.

The old signs are gone, replaced by a mess of false routes and dead ends. Nothing feels certain. Each step brings new choices; each choice, a risk. One wrong move and you're off a cliff. Welcome to the climb.

Three paths lay ahead: one shoots up steep and slick, gleaming like a blade; another twists off narrow and tight, hugging the cliff's edge; the third drops into shadow, a black mouth swallowing itself.

I've stared at choices like this before—real ones. Countless times I sat there, thumb hovering over the 'Confirm Purchase' button, drowning in overdue notices and a pile of bills that looked more like threats than invoices. Buying now felt reckless. But putting it off? Maybe worse. Maybe a lifetime of regret. It was always a war between my short-term self and some faint future version of me—screaming for freedom, hoping I'd survive long enough to reach him.

As you scan the options, your eyes catch a glint of metal near the base of the steep path—a rusty anchor, half-buried in the ice, its surface pitted and worn. You stop. The wind cuts through, sharp and indifferent. I drive a fresh anchor into the ice beside you—*thunk, thunk*—metal biting deep. "Which way?" you ask, voice half-lost in the howl. I look at you, then at the paths. "Your call," I say, and hammer another anchor home.

This isn't just a story. This is your life, right now. You've left the system—or at least trying. The 9-to-5 is behind you, the gurus exposed as frauds, the old rules burned up like that hundred-dollar bill. But here's the catch: no one's telling you what's next. Quit your job? Now you've got to pick—freelance, start a business, live off savings? Ditch the bank? Okay, but where's your money going—gold, crypto, under the mattress? Every choice feels like a cliff, and there's no guidebook, no boss, no influencer to nod and say, "This is the one." The system trained you to follow orders, not make decisions. And now, outside it, that freedom feels less like wings and more like a void.

The steep one's a beast—ice-coated, straight up, like going all-in on Bitcoin. It's not smooth jazz—it's punk rock: raw, unfiltered, promising speed but screaming risk. One slip, and you're done. The narrow one's slower, clinging to the mountain's side—safer, maybe, like diversifying, but it could squeeze you out, leave you dangling. The shadow path—hell, you can't even see where it goes. Could be a shortcut, like betting on an altcoin. Could be a grave.

Each one pulls at you, tugging different strings—ambition, caution, curiosity. I stand beside you, coiling rope, saying nothing. The wind's louder now, like it's daring you to move.

You don't. Minutes drag. Your boots root into the ice. "Which way?" you ask again, sharper this time, like I owe you an answer. "Your call," I repeat, quieter. The weight hits—not the pack, not the climb, but this. Choice. No one's pointing left or right. No voices below, no fake guide promising shortcuts. Just you, the mountain, and three unknowns. Your mind spins: *What if I pick wrong? What if I fall? What if I'm not ready?* The old you—the one who waited for permission—crawls back, whispering, “Go down. It’s clearer there.”

It’s not just doubt. It’s muscle memory. Decades of being told what to do—school, job, bills—carved grooves in your brain. Pick a major, they said. Pick a career, they said. But it was always their menu—you just checked the box. Now there’s no menu, no boxes, and your instincts are rusty. You glance back, down the mountain. The plateau from before glints faintly, tempting. The system’s shadow stretches up, offering structure, certainty. You could retrace your steps. Be safe. Be small. Your hand tightens on the rope.

Then—a crack. A shard of ice shifts under your heel, jolting you forward. No time to think. You lunge for the steep path—not because it’s right, but because it’s there. Your hands claw at the slick face, boots scraping for grip. It’s brutal, instant—lungs burning, fingers numb. I’m behind you, rope taut, calling, “Good enough!” The mountain fights back, but you move. One hold, then another. The narrow path fades from sight. The shadow path vanishes in the haze.

You climb higher, clawing the ice. The steepness bites—every inch a war—but the freeze inside cracks open. You chose. You moved. The summit’s a ghost; what matters is the step you just took. The system chained you to wait for ‘perfect,’ but up here, perfect’s a myth—there’s only forward. I slam an anchor into the rock, its ring a heartbeat in the wind. “Keep going,” I growl. You do.

The mountain spares no one who waits for the wind to decide.

The other paths are gone now, swallowed by the mountain's sprawl. Did they lead anywhere? Doesn't matter. This one's yours. The obstacle wasn't the fork—it was standing still. Freedom isn't a map or a promise—it's motion, even when you're blind. You're not sure this path summits. You're not sure you won't fall. But you're sure you're climbing. That's new.

I pause, wiping frost from my hands, and meet your gaze. "Why the anchors?" you ask, your breath puffing out in the frigid air. I nod toward the one below us, its metal glinting in the ice, then tilt my head at the rusty anchor you spotted earlier. "They're for the climbers who come after us," I say, "but they're also here for us now. They prove others have stood where we stand, faced these same heights, and pressed on. It's comforting, isn't it? Knowing we're not alone in this." You glance at me, then back at the path you've carved out, and something shifts in your eyes. This climb isn't just yours anymore—it's part of a greater story, woven with everyone who's dared it before and all who'll follow.

The steep path eases, just a whisper of relief beneath your boots. The air bites thinner, sharper—ice, rock, and endless silence sprawl before you. No tracks. No promises. You're nowhere near the top, wherever that lies. But the void ahead doesn't claw at you anymore—it beckons, fierce and alive. You tighten your grip, step into it. I'm right behind. We climb, because that's all there is. Ahead, the path narrows, and the doubts within grow louder. A choice looms—one you can't avoid.

Climber's Check List

In Chapter 4, the trail splits, and you realize there's no single "right" path. The biggest risk now is freezing in indecision.

1. **Choose a Direction—Take One Action**
   o If you haven't already, buy a **small** amount of Bitcoin ($10–$20) on the exchange you set up in Chapter 1.
   o Document the process (date, amount, how it felt). This anchors your first real step on this new path.

2. **Map Your Own Route**
   o Write down one short-term goal (e.g., "Accumulate $100 in BTC") and one long-term goal (e.g., "Build a hedge against inflation").
   o Don't wait for perfect conditions—start moving.

"With Bitcoin, I say there is no top because when it comes to the dollar, there is no bottom."

—Max Keiser

Chapter 5: The Fog of Self-Doubt

The orange fire drove you by day; the moon lit your escape by night. You were relentless—step after step, muscle memory guiding the climb. Until the fog hit. Thick. Grey. Smothering. A slow suffocation of doubt.

My pace faltered. Each step heavier than the last. “Too late,” whispered the wind. “Too old,” hissed the cold. My thoughts fogged, the path blurred. The climb turned inward.

Everyone remembers their first Bitcoin regret. Heard about it at $10... $100... maybe $1,000—and passed. “Too late,” they thought. So did I.

That same lie still freezes newcomers too—telling them to stay chained while the price climbs.

Once you understand Bitcoin, everything inverts. It's not about Bitcoin having room to grow against fiat—it's about fiat having room to fall. Your dollars become merely a tool to acquire something truly scarce. To convert soft, decaying currency into money hardened by mathematics. The question shifts from 'When do I cash out?' to 'Why would I ever go back to a system designed to bleed me dry?'

In 2015, I shrugged at $200 Bitcoin. Those coins? Worth a house now. But that sting? It's fuel—because the real tragedy isn't missing the past. It's freezing today while fiat bleeds you dry.

Truth is, Bitcoin has no top because the dollar has no bottom. Quit crying about yesterday's price and start climbing—before tomorrow makes today look cheap.

'It's too late' is no excuse to not store, right now, in the harder money. It's no excuse to not climb—it's the ultimate fiat lie, our own mental trap, engineered to keep us disheartened and unwilling to try again. The moment you see through this, everything transforms: you stop measuring missed opportunities in decaying dollars. Instead, you stack what's real—one sat at a time—because the mountain will still be there tomorrow, unforgiving but patient, waiting for those who finally understand.

Bitcoin looks impossible from the bottom—so most settle for the cage they know.

But you? You've started. As morning crept in, fog still thick as mud, you didn't care. You packed the tent—wet, heavy—and decided to move anyway. The path was gone, but the plan was simple: stack sats slowly.

Eventually, the gray will split. For now, you trusted the dirt under your heels—one mean, blind slog at a time.

The fog stayed stubborn, it didn't matter. Late was an illusion, a blinding trick. Too late to stack, too late to fight, too late to live—fuck that. Muscle memory drove you forward, and your orange dreams lit the escape.

Bitcoin's no fairy tale—it's foggy, and we were in it. Each crunch of ice was a fuck-you to doubt, a promise to keep stacking, to keep climbing.

Every Bitcoiner bleeds the same regret—whether they hesitated at $1 or $50k. The sting is fuel. We're not chasing quick gains; we're stacking something solid.

Trying to shortcut your way to "more" usually just costs you. I used to trade Bitcoin and altcoins—drawing lines all over the charts like I actually knew what I was doing. Support here, resistance there, RSI oversold — felt like I had a map. But most days I was just guessing with extra steps. Hours spent tweaking charts, convincing myself it was strategy — when really, I was just scared to hold. I didn't even understand what it was I was holding. And was eager to "cash out" for a profit.

Took me years to learn: holding isn't weakness. It's defiance. A stance. A middle finger to every fake signal, every distraction designed to knock you off the path.

You missed cheap sats? So did we all. We climb anyway. Stack what's real. One sat at a time.

Climber's Check List

In Chapter 5, self-doubt and regret fog your skull, hissing you're too late. Smash back—know your truth and swing.

1. **Scratch Your Why**
    - Snag a scrap—paper, napkin, anything. Scrawl why you're here—your Bitcoin spit at fiat's grave. Keep it rough, keep it yours. Stash it where regret'll choke on it.

2. **Move, You Bastard**
    - Fog stalling you? Do one thing—anything. Tip a friend a sat. Buy a coffee with BTC, even if it costs more. Movement > paralysis.

"Bitcoin is a tool for underdogs."

—Naval Ravikant

Chapter 6: Shaky Bridge

Your mountain ascent has reached an unavoidable point—a bridge of splintered planks and fraying ropes, hovering over a void where the river's roar devours all light. You step onto the first board—its timbers groan under your weight, sending a shiver up your spine. Below, the dark torrent churns like a beast hungry for your doubt. You lean forward, half-expecting the rope to snap; it quivers in your hands. "Cross or don't. The choice is yours," I murmur, my voice drifting across the emptiness as the bridge sways ominously beneath you.

Each step sends planks groaning. Ropes shudder---a frail promise. Your mind spins: What if Bitcoin tanks? What if my wallet empties overnight? Below, the river churns like a starving beast, ready to devour your courage. "What if I lose it all?" The question hammers with each creak of the bridge. You glance at me for solace. I hold your gaze---an unmoving witness. No one will save you. Only you, this bridge, and your decision.

Then, without warning, the third plank gives way. Your foot plunges into nothingness. You clutch at the frayed ropes; your hands burn as you scramble to keep hold of the bridge. Your heart pounds as you whisper, "Still here." Even as Bitcoin stumbles—a hack, a sudden dip, an unforeseen mishap—you do not abandon the bridge. Others might sell, might run; not you. You cling on, pressing forward, the other side beckoning like a promise of redemption.

And then—bam. In a heart-stopping instant, the bridge gives way. A deafening crack; the ropes snap, and the planks collapse beneath you. You are falling, your scream swallowed by the roar of the plunge. The Bitcoin flag rips from your pack, orange fabric torn free, spinning into the icy water as it slams into your body, the cold stabbing like knives. The shock rips a gasp from your throat, and water races in, filling your lungs as rocks assault your ribs. The current pulls you under—a brutal echo of Bitcoin's sudden downturn, merciless as a market crash that guts your gains in an instant, with no warning. In that freefall, fear and failure intertwine.

The raging water slams you into branches. Broken trees. Laced together, a whole fucking pile of them, ripped from the mountain. You grab on, desperate. The current wants you dead, but the whole tangled mess holds you somehow.

The pile spins. You're on a shit raft in a nightmare. Your blurred vision half makes out my leap from the bank—a desperate lunge that barely makes it. My arms lock around the same thick branches, coughing up half the river.

"Still here?" I yell.

You spit river, nod. The Bitcoin flag—somehow still tangled in your pack—whips behind you. Orange against white death.

The river owns you now. Rocks blast past. Ice chunks crack against the logs. You're not climbing. You're just meat holding onto wood. But your fingers won't let go. Can't let go.

The test wasn't the bridge. Never was.

The test was smashing face-first into freezing hell, body screaming, the mountain trying to kill you, but still gripping on. Still refusing to fucking let go.

While fiat may give the illusion of safety — Bitcoin is the danger that frees you. And you're neck-deep in it.

Wallets can bleed out—hacked. Keys can vanish—gone. One slip—a bad trade, a slick scam—and you're tumbling, nothing to grab.

One particular stuff-up I remember well was simply sending part of my stack one night to the wrong address. No warning. No second chance. Just gone. I had no one to complain to. No one to blame. It was my mistake—and Bitcoin, well, it just kept chugging along like nothing had happened, while I stared at the screen, gut hollow, as if the floor had dropped out beneath me.

You feel that same hollow now, don't you? Out here, the current doesn't pause for your panic.

Bitcoin is for underdogs. And right now, half-dead in the icy cold, you embody that stubbornness. You're not a fancy trader. Not an investor. Just meat that won't quit.

The protocol grinds on while you cling to driftwood, alive

or dead. That's the point—you're not begging it to save you. You're saving yourself. One frozen finger at a time.

Climber's Check List

In Chapter 6, you face your deepest fears: market crashes, hacks, the terror of losing it all. The key lesson: falling isn't the end—getting back up is.

1. **Prepare for a Fall**
   o Write down one specific action you'll take if Bitcoin's price tanks. (Example: "I'll hold at least 3 months before making any decision," or "I'll buy a little more at lower prices.")
   o Having this plan in place keeps panic at bay when fear hits.

2. **Lock It Down**
   o Set up a hardware wallet, then write your recovery seed on paper... or chisel it into steel! And stash it somewhere safe. That's your Bitcoin lifeboat.

"For people who have dedicated their lives to help bitcoin succeed like myself, it's time to refuel and store energy for the long journey ahead."

—Wences Casares

Chapter 7: Base Camp

The river spits us out—our branches slamming into a jut of rock. We scramble off, clawing for something—anything—solid. My boots find grip first. I turn, grab your arm, haul you up. We collapse on the ledge, heaving, soaked, alive.

Orange light flickers off stone. A fire. Real warmth—not ideology, not conviction—just heat. Shapes move around it. Scarred hands. Steaming mugs. Quiet laughter. Other climbers.

I hang back, checking gear, catching my breath. But you—you need that fire.

You limp toward it, dripping, Bitcoin flag clutched like its proof you belong. But it's not the flag they see—it's your shredded pack, your bloodied hands, your thousand-yard stare. The mountain's signature, written in pain.

A woman looks up, older, eyes sharp. Takes in your damage with one glance. She pats the ground beside her. No words needed. Your broken body is all the credentials required here.

You collapse, shivering.

"First time?" she asks, eyeing your shredded pack.

You nod.

"Bridge gets everyone," she says. "Or the fog. Or... If you're here, you're one of us."

They call this place Base Camp.

Not the summit. Not safety. Just a momentary stillness between hells. Like when Bitcoin runs from $3k to $20k and everyone thinks they're a genius. A breather. A trap, if you confuse it for the end.

Someone passes you coffee. Bitter. Strong. It hurts going down. It helps.

Around you—maybe a dozen others. Different stages of the climb. Some pristine, some wrecked. One guy's missing two fingers. Another sketches multisig setups in the dirt. The woman beside you sips like it's medicine.

"Panic sold," she says with a smirk. "Bought back at double. Doesn't matter. Price wasn't the point. Still here."

Stories flow with the smoke. A mother speaks softly of her daughter—eight years old. "I want her to grow up where her time means something. Where her future isn't borrowed from someone else's debt." A developer recounts the day his bank froze his account for daring to buy freedom. A teacher admits she spent two decades saving into a pension that turned out to be numbers on paper—backed by nothing but political promises. One kid, far too young to be climbing, stares into the fire. “I started with memes,” he says. “Now I’d die on this hill.”

You’re taken back. “You don’t have to be climbing...”

The woman replies without looking at you. "There's nothing left down there, he climbs if he wants. Plus, he’s better with the tech than most of us"

Silence spreads. Heavy, not sad.

Above, stars blink through the thinning clouds. Constant little flickers of light.

One of the newer climbers—his gear barely marked—pulls a cracked phone from a plastic bag, glances at the screen, and announces the current price.

A few grunts. Someone spits into the fire.

"Rather not hear it, mate," the woman beside you says. Not angry. Just tired.

He puts his phone away, confused. "But we're winning..."

"Price goes up, price goes down," she cuts him off. "We're still on the same fucking mountain."

The guy missing fingers laughs, bitter. "Last bull run, I thought I was a genius. This time? I stack and shut up."

Heads nod in agreement.

You sit straighter, looking around. This isn't a rest. This is preparation.

One guy hunches near the fire, slamming a steel punch into a metal plate—his cold wallet etched into permanence with each strike. He uses a rock as a hammer. No hesitation. No do-overs. Another kneels in the dirt, scratching out a rough plan—what to sell, what to cut, how to stack harder next month. A quiet man mutters mantra to himself, "Not your keys, not your wallet."

You join in, placing the flag—tattered and damp—near the fire to dry out. For a second, everyone watches it. The fabric. The color.

A younger climber shifts beside you. "Think you'll be the one to make it?"

You glance at the flag, the fire, then the stars. A flicker of unease hits—because you know damn well you can't summit alone. But knowing this tribe exists—same fight, same goals—changes everything.

I come over and give you a nod. You shoulder your pack and call out, "See you at the top."

The woman beside us shakes her head. "Avoid those bridges—otherwise you'll be back here." She laughs.

We turn from the fire and step onto the unbroken path, leaving the others behind.

You test your gear. Stretch your legs. The blizzard's

building. You can feel it.

"Ready?" I ask.
You nod. "Let's climb."

The fire dies behind us, but the warmth stays in your chests.

Climber's Check List

In Chapter 7, you find community. This is where conviction is sharpened—not by price, but by principle.

1. **Fortify Your Setup**
    - Cold storage in place?
    - Backups written and protected?
2. **Find Your Tribe**
    - Join one Bitcoin community this week
    - Share your story, hear others
    - Base Camp is everywhere climbers gather
3. **Share the Fire**
    - Tell someone about your climb
    - Share what you've learned—strength spreads fastest at base camp

"Every day that goes by and Bitcoin hasn't collapsed due to legal or technical problems, that brings new information to the market. It increases the chance of Bitcoin's eventual success and justifies a higher price."

—Hal Finney

Chapter 8: The Blizzard of Doubt

We climb in silence. No words. Just frost and rising tension.

The mountain goes quiet, holding its breath.
You feel it—not just in the air, but in your gut. That primal alert. The same feeling prey get seconds before the trap snaps. A chill rolls down your spine. The calm before the storm.

The first gust tears at your cheeks, a bitter warning. "Anchor down—now," I shout over the rising wind. No argument. You feel it coming: a storm designed to crush.

Before you secure the last strap, the blizzard hits—no ordinary storm. It's a coordinated attack, hitting every Bitcoiner sooner or later. The wind carries voices, smug media pundits chanting the "end of crypto." Snow blinds you, flakes carrying lies, rewriting reality. Your phone buzzes wildly—friends sharing news of exchange collapses, simultaneous crackdowns in multiple countries, market charts bleeding red.

This isn't mere doubt. It's a sophisticated, timed assault, striking at your weakest moment. In this blinding whiteout, isolation is deadly—you can't see the thousands battling the same storm. You clutch the rope, teeth clenched, every nerve screaming panic. It feels like that crumbling bridge again, but this time there's nowhere to run.

Headlines whip past like icy gusts:

- "Bitcoin Banned!"

- "Exchange Crash!"

- "BITCOIN—IT'S DEAD!"

Each scream tries to erase what you know, freezing you in place. The cold penetrates, whispering you're insane, destined to lose it all. Your grip tightens, mind spinning in the relentless wind: Am I mad to keep climbing? You remember the bridge—how you nearly turned back. This is that moment, all over again, only now there's no edge in sight. No fall to escape to. Just climb—or collapse.

The storm howls louder, offering no comfort. You glance at me; our eyes lock—grim determination in both, pure grit.

Your anchor bites—cold steel backed by colder conviction. Keys offline, automated buys immune to panic. The storm roars, but your setup remains silent, indifferent.

Your deeper strength isn't visible; it's forged in nights spent decoding Satoshi's whitepaper line by line—when "21 million" finally clicked and you understood Bitcoin's true purpose. You've studied survivors' tales of brutal crashes and tracked hash rate climbing, unphased by every "Bitcoin is dead" headline.

For me, I built resilience by diving into monetary history—understanding why Bitcoin exists and what problems with fiat it's trying to solve.

I learnt about shells and rai stones, and I wrote books like Bitcoin or Death and Hardest Money Wins to force that knowledge into me. To anchor me, when the real storms hit.

When news screams of another "China ban," you smile, recalling Bitcoin's stubborn survival through every past attempt.

The wind screams louder, memories flood back—the crash of 2018, Bitcoin plunging from $20k to $3k, the world declaring it dead. 2014, when Mt. Gox imploded, wiping out half the ecosystem. Every blizzard buried weak hands. Every spring revealed survivors whose anchors held firm.

Your grip tightens further. The storm tests, but you've weathered worse. Time and again, pundits declared Bitcoin's death. Yet here you are—no guru, no cheering crowd, just fierce resolve that your anchors will hold.

Slowly, gradually, the wind eases. Snow thins. The storm doesn't vanish instantly but fades, exhausted.

Hours later—or maybe days—the sky cracks open, pale sun piercing through, cautious at first, then boldly warming your frozen limbs. Stiff muscles thaw, hopes reignite. I exhale shakily, laughing in relief and disbelief.

You've changed. Not just hardened—clarified. The noise that used to pierce you now passes through like wind through wire mesh. You don't react. You recognize. The FUD that once crippled you feels almost... boring. A tired playbook. Our eyes meet again, tired but unwavering. "Still climbing?" I ask, knowing the answer. You nod, slight smile emerging.

The mountain isn't conquered yet. The storms will return. But now the sun shines, your dreams alive once more. When the next blizzard hits, you'll be ready—anchors set, mind sharp, resolve hardened. You step forward, sure-footed, not despite the storm, but strengthened because of it.

Climber's Check List

In Chapter 8, the storm was meant to break you. Instead, it tempered you. Hold your ground and strengthen your anchors:

1. **Reinforce Your Anchor**
   o Revisit the core reasons you started this climb—your research, your belief in Bitcoin's fundamentals.
   o Remind yourself that storms (bear markets, negative headlines) have come and gone before, and each time, the mountain still stood.

2. **Freeze Out FUD**
   o Avoid the dramatized headlines.

"Trusted third parties are security holes."

—Nick Szabo

Chapter 9:
False Summit

The air thins, something shifts. A ridge looms ahead, sharp against the fog. Your hopes tighten—could this be it? You speed up, boots scraping ice, breath shallow. The end's in sight. You're sure of it. I lag behind, rope taut between us. You don't wait—claw yourself over the edge, hand extended back to drag me up.

We made it. You feel it in your bones.

Your boots hit flat ground, sudden stability beneath your feet. Your lungs fill, relief surging—until you look up. Hope evaporates quicker than a shitcoin pump. No summit here, just a mocking plateau. The real peak rises beyond, colder, steeper, shrouded in brutal mist.

"Fuck," you mutter, fists clenching. The wind laughs coldly. This isn't it. Not even close.

Dropping to your knees, your eyes lock onto frozen bodies scattered around, eyes wide in permanent shock, mouths twisted into hollow smiles—success frozen into eternal mockery. I kneel beside one, prying loose a leather wallet from stiff fingers. Platinum credit cards, investment statements, property deeds spill out—everything the world calls "success," now meaningless in death.

Reality hits not like a punch, but like a slow, poisonous revelation. These weren't climbers who failed—these were climbers who succeeded, at the wrong summit.

"These weren't typical failures," I say, voice hollow. "They genuinely believed they'd escaped. That one was a millionaire trader, rich in fiat until it meant nothing. She built a real estate empire but lost everything when taxes tripled overnight. That guy—startup millionaire, his eight-figure exit evaporated by inflation. They thought they'd beaten the system, but the system owned them all along."

Stacking cash, stocks, or real estate might make you rich—but if you're still counting in dollars, you haven't escaped; you're just playing the same rigged game at a higher level. True escape means measuring your worth in something untouchable by politicians, immune to inflation, and indifferent to financial crises.

The mountain doesn't care about your ego. One smug second, and it'll chew you up faster than you climbed.

You stare at the bodies preserved up here, glassy eyes locked onto nothing.

“Who were they?” you rasp.

I shake my head, voice sharp. “The cocky ones. They thought they’d won because they changed jobs, banked cash, flipped real estate. Thought they’d found shortcuts. Then inflation gutted their cash, markets wrecked their stocks, and governments seized their property. They stopped climbing, thinking the system couldn’t touch them anymore—and that’s when it swallowed them whole.”

I pause, voice low.

“Now they’re just warnings for us.”

You swallow, gut twisting.

You kick a rock into the void, frustration burning your throat. "Thought we were done with this shit," you mutter, anger mixed with exhaustion.

I shake my head, staring up towards the real peak in the distance.

This mountain never stops testing. Bitcoin doesn’t either. One moment of pride, one second you think you’re beyond its reach, it crushes you. Those frozen faces thought they’d made it. Look at them now—smug, lifeless, trapped forever.

You stand slowly, eyes locked on the climb ahead.

"How much more?"

"Enough to break us," I reply.

You grunt, stepping forward. I follow.

The false summit's behind us—a lesson etched in ice: comfort kills, arrogance buries you. Rope taut. Wind fierce. We climb.

Climber's Check List

The fake summit's a trap—don't strut. Stay humble, stay hungry.

1. **Find Your Illusion**
    - Write down one area where you think you've "escaped" but might still be dependent on the system.
    - Be brutal. Are you still measuring wealth in fiat? **Are you still** working for cash instead of sovereignty?

2. **Stay Uncomfortable**

    - Comfort is the enemy. If you feel like you've "made it," find a new challenge.

"Stay humble. Stack sats."

—Matt Odell

Chapter 10: The High Ledge

The mountain's a monster now—ice-slick, wind howling like it wants us gone. We're high. Too high to turn back. Summit's now a gray smear through the fog. You're crouched on a narrow ledge, breath ragged, hands numb. I'm beside you, wrestling a rope into a crevice. My jacket's shredded, flapping useless. I ditch it. Cold rakes me, but we've got to move.

You glance over, eyes sharp despite the freeze. My shirt's torn—chest and side bared. A scar catches you, jagged, carved along my side. Your eyes follow it up, your hand lifting my shirt away. "What the hell?" you rasp, the scars crisscrossing my body, deep, thick. I keep at the rope, knotting tight. "Old scratches," I grunt. You don't buy it.

Leave it alone," I snap, but you're not letting go. Your hand's on my side—cold, steady—already tracing another scar, then another, lines clawing a map across my chest and ribs, a ledger of pain under your fingers. I flinch, shame scorching through the chill.

"These all from the obstacles?" you ask, voice low.

I hang my head. "Yeah," I mutter. "Hit each one. More than I like to admit." I glance down, hand brushing a thick ridge. “They’re not just fuck-ups. They’re the map out.”

“Cloud mining,” I mutter. “Smaller and smaller returns, until you couldn’t even withdraw. No proof they were mining anything—just a Ponzi with a login screen.”
I shake my head. “Fell for bullshit.”

You slide to a gnarled mark near my collar. “Shitcoins. Chased the hype, lost it all.”

A long scar across my ribs. “ICOs,” I mutter. “Whitepapers, fake roadmaps, hype videos… nothing but pump & dumps.” I let out a dry laugh. “Most never even had a product.”

A gouge down my side. “Chasm. Keys gone. Months of stacking—wiped.”

Then you find it—the worst one. Raw, ridged, twisted beneath my ribs. I flinch.

“Bitconnect,” I say, voice flat. “The biggest scar of mine.”

I stare out past the ledge. “They promised daily gains. Compounding in fact. Big events. Suits. Influencers hyping it like gospel. Said it was foolproof.”

I exhale hard.

“Then one day—white page. Site gone. Just echoes now.”

My voice drops to a bitter rasp: “Bitcoooonneeect…”

This isn't just mountain fiction. Every scar in this chapter is real. I earned them the hard way—and most Bitcoiners share the same pain.

Bitconnect alone stole $2.4 billion from dreamers chasing 1% daily returns. Cloud mining? Countless operations vanished with investor funds, leaving behind dead sites. And shitcoins—the graveyard's endless. For every Bitcoin success story, there are dozens of cautionary tales carved in flesh and bank statements.

The brutal truth: Bitcoin's learning curve has no safety net. Traditional finance hides its failures behind bailouts and insurance. Bitcoin exposes everything—every hack, every scam, every moment of weakness becomes public blockchain history. That transparency terrifies newcomers, but it's also Bitcoin's greatest teacher. The community's collective scars become everyone's roadmap.

You stop, your palm still throbbing where the bridge collapse carved its own mark. In that pulse of pain, you understand—this scarred path through this mountain's teeth will be yours too. You trace that jagged line with your finger, your first real wound from the climb. The pain is raw, immediate, but you're still here. Still standing. Still ready to push forward.

“Listen,” I say, turning to face you, eyes locked. “If I don't make it—if this ice cracks, or the wind wins—you keep going. I'll be fine. You don't stop. Not for me. Not for any shit. Okay?” Your jaw tightens, guilt still there, but you nod.

Wind screams. We don't turn back. You look down at your palm again, the cut from the bridge still weeping.
"More scars coming," you mutter.
I nod, "Freedom leaves scars."

The mountain's unforgiving. No room for ego. Just scars, grit, and stacked sats.

I test the rope—taut. "Ready?" The summit's a shadow, close but cruel. You stand, slow. "Okay."
I grab my gear. We climb. Marked and all.

Climber's Check List

Your scars are proof you're in the fight. Learn fast, or the mountain wins.

1. **Own Your Scar**
    - Write down one Bitcoin mistake you've made (e.g., "Fell for a scam," "Lost my seed phrase"). Flip it—what's the lesson? (e.g., "Vet everything," "Back up my keys"). Keep that note where you'll see it.

2. **Prep for the Solo Stretch**
    - Pick one way to stay strong if you're left alone (e.g., "Join a Bitcoin crew," "Save a solid resource link"). Set it up this week.

"Bitcoin is the only asset capable of addressing the root cause of currency debasement and recurring market meltdowns."

—Preston Pysh

Chapter 11: All Obstacles at Once

You're clawing your way up the mountain, the peak looming like a cruel mirage. Every step's a fight—your boots sinking, lungs burning, hands numb. You're close, so damn close. Then it hits: a low rumble turns into a deafening roar. The avalanche crashes down—snow, ice, and rock thundering toward you, unstoppable. You dive for cover, but it's useless. The white wall slams you under.

Your body tumbles in the chaos. Up becomes down. Left becomes right. The roar deafens you, bones crack against hidden rocks. Then—the movement stops. Snow settles. Dead silence.

Now it's your prison. Snow floods your mouth, your nose. The weight crushes your chest, pins your legs. You can't breathe. Can't move. The mountain's fury has buried you completely. Just cold, suffocating dark.

The cold cuts through gear, through skin, straight into bone. Your lungs claw for oxygen. Your muscles lock. This is the trap. Not neat. Not controlled. Just chaos—brutal, merciless, all at once.

Bitcoin's avalanche looks like this: You wake up 30% in the red. Your wife finds the credit card statement from your last buy. China bans Bitcoin (again). Your brother-in-law forwards you that Warren Buffett video again, where he's calling Bitcoin rat poison. The bank calls about 'suspicious activity.' Your stomach drops. Your hands shake. You can't breathe. This is it—the full weight of every doubt you ever had, plus everyone else's, crushing your chest at 3AM when you're too tired to fight back.

You had two options, prepare for the avalanches or survive them raw.

The prepared ones already secured their keys offline, set automatic purchases, built conviction through knowledge—not price action. They sidestep a lot of the panic by staying detached from the storm's pull.

The unprepared? They live through every brutal second—sleepless nights, the doubt, the full weight crushing their chest. But if they don't sell, if they hold through the suffocation, they emerge scarred but stronger.

Both paths lead up the mountain. One's calculated. One's pure pain.

You chose pain. I've felt this weight. The charts red. YouTubers silent—or getting arrested. Telegrams turning toxic. I'd watch, as my portfolio halved, then halved again. A trading course I'd sunk money into? Useless. And the "community"? Felt like it had vanished the second the hype dried up.

That's when I almost bailed. Not just from Bitcoin—from

the whole damn idea of freedom.

But here's the truth: you're not buried under chaos because you picked Bitcoin. You picked Bitcoin because the world is chaotic. Climbing broke you—but staying in that old world would've buried you completely. You didn't choose the easy path. You chose the only one that fights back.

Reaching for me, you find nothing. Just more snow. More cold. You're utterly alone. The panic rises—sharp as a blade. Each second without air stretches like an hour. Your mind flashes with brutal clarity: wallets never backed up. Seeds left vulnerable. All your work—about to die with you, buried under tons of indifferent white.

I yell your name, but the snow swallows it. Somewhere nearby, you're fighting too—or maybe you're not. I can't tell. The snow keeps piling. Heavier. Colder. My arms go slack. The silence creeps in—no shouts, no wind, just a thick, final stillness.

I'm yelling muffled pleas through the snow: *"HODL! FUCKIN' HODL!"* But there's only silence in return. The words choke in the frozen void, buried beneath the weight, unanswered.

The mountain doesn't care.

Your lungs empty. Your heartbeat slows. Consciousness flickers—like Bitcoin's orange flame guttering out. The cold presses harder. The fight fades. And the dream slips away.

Nothing but stillness.
Nothing but dark.
Nothing.

Climber's Check List

Chaos hits hard. In Bitcoin, you don't break—you bend and keep climbing.

1. **Build Your Crash Kit**
    - Write down three actions for a 50% drop: Re-read what you wrote down for your 'Why Escape' in Chapter 1, text my hodler buddy, Unplug for 24 hours.

2. **Ban Price Checks**
    - Commit to one week without looking at Bitcoin's price. Instead, read Bitcoin books. Feel the calm of ignoring the storm.

"Bitcoin links together 8 billion people, links together a hundred million companies, it synchronizes the world across political jurisdictions, and it returns rationality to the entire financial system, and it returns freedom and property rights to the entire human race."

—Michael Saylor

Chapter 12: The Edge of the Unknown

Darkness. Complete. Final.

Then—a pinprick.

Orange pierces the void, impossibly distant at first, then expanding. Not light—heat. Raw, demanding heat forcing its way through frozen veins. Death isn't done with you. Or maybe you're not done with life. Your fist punches through the snow, bloody, shaking. "HODL!" still echoing, the word a gut-punch as we rip free from the avalanche's grip. The mountain threw everything at us—snow, rock, death. It lost. We're up, barely.

Ropes tightened, we now don't waste a breath. We climb. Two bodies fighting the mountain's wrath. Slick ice shatters. Jagged rock cuts deep. Wind screams for blood. We don't stop.

Below us, fiat's world burns. Banks collapse. Currencies die. Wars rage over paper. The chaos nips at our heels, but we're outpacing it.

No ledge? No problem. My boot digs into your hip. Your hand locks on my leg. We form a human ladder. Trust made flesh. The summit taunts us. Close. Brutal. Unforgiving. Every step tempts death. We take it anyway.

That fire from day one still burns. Hotter now. Fed by every battle won. The bridge collapse. The fake guide. The blizzard of FUD. Fake summits. Each scar earned. Each obstacle crushed. Pure fuel pushing us towards freedom.

Fingers find impossible holds, ice cracking under my grip as I haul myself higher. You watch, study, then follow, matching my movements with near-perfect precision. Our breaths sync—white clouds puffing rhythmically in the thin air. The rope between us hangs slack, no longer a lifeline but a symbol of how far we've come. Our eyes lock briefly, a silent acknowledgment. The summit waits, so close, we can almost taste its bitter victory.

Then it happens.

Crack!

The rock I was holding, flies past your head. Tumbling into darkness. I claw for new grip. My feet slip.

I fall.

Plummeting past you. A flash of panic. The rope snaps tight. Whips hard. Yanks you off balance. My full weight—body, gear, fear—slams through our lifeline.

The metal anchor screams against the ice, bending but refusing to surrender. Your body becomes the fulcrum between my life and death, your shoulder grinding against jagged rock as the force tears through muscle and bone. White-hot explosion of pain rips a strangled sound from your throat. Below, I dangle in empty space, swinging over the abyss. The rope stretches, fibers straining audibly. Ice crystals shower down, catching sunlight as they fall past me into nothingness—beautiful and terrifying, like the journey that brought us here.

The mountain holds its breath. Your grip tightens, knuckles bleached white against the blood-red rope. Not letting go. Not even thinking about it. I kick wildly at the void, searching for help, where there is none. The wind doesn't just howl now—it laughs, a cold mockery of my desperation. Nothing between me and oblivion but your locked joints and that screaming anchor.

"Keep going," I shout, each word scraped raw by the thin air, by the truth I've known since we started this climb.

You roar back, all fury and defiance, spittle freezing on your lips: "No! We're doing this together!" Your fists clench the rope like it's stitched to your soul.

But below, I'm already working—fingers numb but precise. One strand parts, the knife slicing through like butter, two strands, the rope thinning between us. Not from panic. From purpose.

"Your escape!" I lock eyes with you, pouring everything into that final gaze—all the falls, all the scars, all the reasons we climbed in the first place.

You see it before it happens. You know, even as you reject it.

The last strand surrenders with nothing more than a whisper, and I drop—not falling but diving into the darkness that's always been waiting.

Your scream follows me down, tearing through the mountain until your voice breaks. Then silence.

You're alone.

Tears stream down your face, freezing almost instantly, tiny diamonds of grief locked in time. You grip the frayed end of the rope, knuckles white, chest heaving with sobs that tear at your ribs. *Your escape*. My words burn in your skull, bitter and undeniable. This climb, this fight—you've been left to finish — alone.

You curse under your breath, rage and grief tangling in your throat, but beneath it, a flicker of realization ignites: this is what true escape demands. Complete sovereignty. No guides. No safety nets. Just you, your beliefs, your convictions.

You face the final wall—ice and stone, slick and merciless. Boots scrape, fingers bleed, lungs claw at thin air. No cushion, just the peak that's tried to kill you at every step. Hours bleed out, silent and bitter. Then, the peak. No more up. Just sky.

You stand, legs shaking, fists balled against the cold. Below, chaos sprawls small. Above, orange sky burns infinite. You've made it. But it's not yours—it hits you, heavy as hell.

Your fingers, bloody and stiff, fumble with the zipper of your pack. You dig deep, past survival gear and rations, until you feel it—the fabric I pressed into your hands what feels like a lifetime ago. You pull the orange, torn, sweat-soaked Bitcoin flag free. You stare at it, then at your ravaged backpack. With a grunt, you tear at the frame, ripping the aluminium support rod from the pack's spine. It takes three attempts, your frozen hands slipping on the metal, but finally it breaks free.

You stand, flag and makeshift pole in hand. Then with a roar that carries all your effort, you slam it into the ice—the sound of mankind's work echoing across the summit. Orange fabric snaps taut in the wind, blazing defiance against the fiat world below. This isn't a win—it's proof. Hard money, verified through every fall, every brutal effort that brought you back up.

Underfoot, the mountain stacked with the dead—coders burned out, rebels gutted, traders bartering shells, smiths forging gold, dreamers chasing something solid. They bled and broke for this, block by block across time. Bitcoin's ours because they paid for it.

And then it lands: this climb, this flag—it's not your escape. It's for everyone. All of them. Every soul still trapped down there, clawing for a way out. You fought for yourself, but finished for them.

No speeches. Just the rope, coiled and frayed in your hands. Below—banks collapse, savings vanish, the world burns. But you're steady. Your eyes blaze orange now—focused, unshakable. Ice, lies, fear—none of it stops you. You climbed for yourself. Now you fight for those still crushed by fiat below.

Gear cinched, you descend. The mission's clear now—bring others up. Friends. Family. Everyone still trapped. Help them escape. Because the climb was never just for you.

Climber's Check List

1. **Lead the Way** - Bitcoin's bigger than you. Teach a friend about Bitcoin, help them up the mountain. Get them started today.

EPILOGUE: The Climb Continues

You've busted your ass to get here—survived the void, battled the blizzard, planted that orange flag. But this isn't the finish line. The system below still grinds lives into dust. Your escape was never just yours.

Bitcoin is more than money—it's a blazing signal fire. It's the map up and the rope back. Planting the flag doesn't end the fight. It begins the mission. Every sat you stack, every node you run, carves a clearer path for someone still stuck in the churn.

Now you descend, not to rest but to guide. You carry your scars like compasses, your stories like torches. You become the climber you needed when you stared at your first peak—terrified, skeptical, desperate for a way out.

Here's the kicker: the mountain gets easier with every new climber. Each wallet secured, each seed phrase backed up, each sceptical friend convinced, makes the next ascent smoother. Freedom isn't a solo sprint; it's a relay. A joint effort. A grind built on years of trying.

Your next mission: pick one person still trapped—roommate, co-worker, distant cousin—and hand them this book today. Not tomorrow. Today. Every day they wander in the fog, the system siphons more hours of their life.

You felt that rush at the summit. Don't let them roam in darkness when you wield the light. Extend your rope. Shout the coordinates. Put this book in their hands.

What are you waiting for? Lace up. Move. Bring them up. The climb never ends. But damn, it's worth it.

CLIMBER'S GEAR: ESSENTIAL EQUIPMENT FOR YOUR ESCAPE

BASIC CAMP GEAR (GETTING STARTED)

Mobile Wallets – Your first shelter

- Muun Wallet: Simple, non-custodial wallet for beginners
- Blue Wallet: More advanced features while maintaining simplicity
- Setup Time: 10 minutes. Security Level: Basic but better than exchanges

Security Fundamentals -- Your first defence line

- Create a unique email used only for Bitcoin accounts
- Use a password manager (Bitwarden or 1Password) to generate and store complex, unique passwords
- Schedule monthly security audits: check for exchange withdrawal address whitelisting, confirm backup accessibility and verify authentication apps are synced correctly

- Threat model practice: Spend one hour mapping what could go wrong with your setup and create one specific action to address each vulnerability

Exchange Accounts – Base camp supplies

- Kraken, Coinbase, or local equivalent
- Use only for purchasing, not long-term storage
- Enable maximum security features (2FA with authenticator app, never SMS)
- Security Tip: Never keep more than one month's DCA amount on an exchange

Learning Resources – Your map

- Bitcoin whitepapers (beginner-friendly versions available)
- "The Bitcoin Standard" by Saifedean Ammous
- "Inventing Bitcoin" by Yan Pritzker (shorter, technical introduction)
- Andreas Antonopoulos videos for clear, trustworthy explanations

MID-MOUNTAIN EQUIPMENT (INTERMEDIATE SECURITY)

Hardware Wallets – Your anchors against storms

- Trezor Model One: Simple, open-source hardware security
- Ledger Nano S Plus: Alternative with secure element
- Setup Time: 1 hour. Security Level: Strong

Metal Seed Storage – Protection from elements

- Coldbit Steel: Punch plate for seed phrase backup
- Cobo Tablet: Modular metal storage solution
- Security Tip: Store in multiple locations, never together with your device

Node Setup – Self-reliance tools

- Umbrel or RaspiBlitz: For running your own Bitcoin node
- Setup Time: 1 day. Technical Level: Moderate
- Benefit: Verification without trusting third parties

SUMMIT EQUIPMENT (ADVANCED SOVEREIGNTY)

Multisignature Setup – Ropes that won't break

- Sparrow Wallet + multiple hardware devices
- Requires 2-of-3 or 3-of-5 signatures to move funds
- Setup Time: 1 weekend. Security Level: Fort Knox

Cold Storage – Protection from all elements

- Air-gapped computers running Electrum
- Paper wallets (for smaller amounts only)
- Hardware wallets stored in tamper-evident bags

Inheritance Planning – Anchors for those who follow

- Dead man's switch protocols
- Shamir's Secret Sharing for distributing keys to trusted parties
- Written instructions for heirs (stored with lawyer or trusted family)

EXPEDITION LEADER GEAR (BRINGING OTHERS UP)

Teaching Tools – For helping newcomers

- Orange Pills: Teach others!
- Gift them knowledge like this very book!
- Practice: Set up test wallets with small amounts
- "Bitcoin for Beginners" local meetup resources

Community Building – Camp supplies for group climbs

- Meetup.com or Telegram groups for local Bitcoin communities
- Nostr for censorship-resistant communication
- Resources for hosting home Bitcoin education sessions

Gifting Bitcoin – Ropes to pull others up

- Paper wallets with small amounts and clear instructions
- Guide for setting up a child's first Bitcoin savings

Remember: No gear is effective without knowledge. Spend as much time learning as you do accumulating. The strongest climbers aren't those with the most equipment—they're those who understand every tool they carry.

Made in the USA
Monee, IL
04 November 2026

67378037R00046